O SONG

Poems & Art

Sharon Webster

ISBN-13: 978-1-967022-12-0
Library of Congress Control Number: 2025951441

Fomite
58 Peru Street
Burlington, VT 05401

02-05-2026

For Dave
and the song tomorrow

PRAISE

"O, what a wonderful book! -- sometimes quirky and exuberant; sometimes tender, elegiac; sometimes dark, raw. But always Sharon Webster *notices things*: the family house *exactly somewhere between a tobacco field and suburbia.* And the crows! *A tree cries/ through the night/ swollen with crows.*"

–Sue D. Burton, author of poetry collections, *Box* and *Little Steel*

O Song is an outpouring of sound in visceral threads where colors cluster below the surface and shine. In this land where *the soft white ghost of our cat/* comes back to watch at the window, Sharon Webster dissolves the boundaries between art and music, making room for the *words in our laps like warm nets.* She sees metaphors for cohesion in well-oiled rituals, cloth and the *ten true moons* of her fingertips. She brings us through the intimate grief of losing a bluegrass-infused brother, past ancestors in the mirror, to alight on branches heavy with crows. Webster's lyricism is a treasured friend from whom *You can part company and not be gone.*"

–Cindy Ellen Hill, author of *Love in a Time of Climate Change*, *Wild Earth*, and *Elegy for the Trees*

THANK YOU

Dave Cavanagh, for infusing almost everything I do with ineffable support and abiding love. What else can I say?

Marc Estrin, unstoppable co-founder of Fomite Press, whose confidence as artist, activist, and facilitator lives on in his many books and people he touched. RIP

Donna Bister, Marc's partner and co-founder of Fomite, whose gifted persistence and talents are alive in every book published by Fomite and continue in this one. The energy is infectious.

Sue Burton, for your ingeniously frisky insights on my manuscript, your sensitivity, humor, and the gift of your time.

Cindy Ellen Hill, for your brilliant copy editing and for sharing your special spark. Sometimes I'm in awe.

Anna Blackmer, for your true heart that refreshes me as a friend, poet, and mentor. I'm so grateful.

Greg Delanty, for your literary support from the beginning. As the first person to suggest that my poems could come live as a book, I say always, thank you!

Tina Escaja, fiery supporter and midwife of art and life. Thank you!

Kim Arney, Daniel Webster, Jeff Webster: you are more than siblings, you are graceful supporters, intelligent consultants, and cheerful accomplices.
Sisters-in-love, Jessica Bernstein, Susan Van Haitsma, and Phyllis Cavanagh, for their keen insights and enduring care.

Chuck Webster, gentle brave brother, for where you took us in our hearts.

These poems were previously published:
"Witness Poem" in *05401*
"Last Night" in *Roads Taken: An Anthology of Vermont Poets*
"Sentinels" in *Kind of a Hurricane*

"Because the Cloth" and "How the Blue of the Chicory" in
PoemTown Anthology, Randolph VT 2024
"A Trick" in *Not That Fastened*
"Black Birds" in PoemCity Montpelier 2024 Anthology
"I Have the Sunset" in *This Fragrance, Too*
"Make Anew" in Poem City Montpelier 2025
"A Tree Cries" and "O song that pulled this wetness" in *Poetic License,* solo art exhibit at *The SPACE Gallery, Burlington VT*
"The Broken Church" and "Living Here" *in Vital Signs, Instigations,* Fomite Press, 2025
"May Third" in PoemCity Montpelier Anthology 2025

Contents

Crows

Parting

About The Author

O Song

O SONG

wind your threads around me, entangle
and chase
me,
chisel me.
Replace me.
Trace me. Mend
and sweep
me, kiss
these prickled
dreams and addendums.
Consume me.
Confuse me. Rhythm,
loosen
and lose me
in patterns with shoulders
and shifts. Enfold
and hold
me in strands of sorrow and bliss.
O song, abide.

FIND YOUR STORIES

remember the ones you remember, young
as you've ever been, wet
in the middle of dried
out bark, yourself
wholly given
to this day
while soft
bubbles cluster below the surface
and shine.

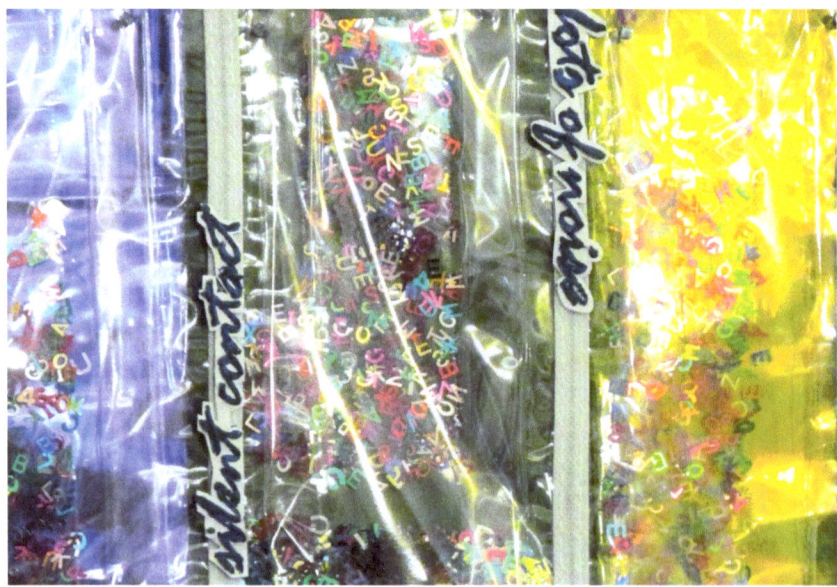

Silent Contact, Lots of Noise , mixed media with foil letters and thread

LAST NIGHT

we made a beautiful life together
                    while the tall trees latched
                    onto the new seeds
                    and the old grass.
                    The moist towels unfolded.
Here is our weathered flagpole, our rope. Here
                    is our back story,
                    the broken pages
                    stitched to the wind
                    that relaxes in drawers
                    and corners, forbidden
                    and forgiven.
Here is the length of the yard where our lives laid down
                    to measure the tendrils
                    and the moist towels.
                    Here is our scorched food
                    and our drudgery.
                    Here
                    is our delicacy
                    to hold up the world
                    tonight.
                    Here is our rickety life
                    raft, our glistening garbage
                    and our laughing.
Here are our well-oiled rituals and our scratchy
enjambments.

Look! Now the soft white ghost
                        of our little cat has
                        come back
                        to wait at the window
                        and watch, his mossy ears
                        listening. A little
                        bit further
                        in the yard, a yellow
                        finch made herself
                    a home
        in the stand of sunflowers
        in the forest of time that we made last night.

Backyard Scene, watercolor crayon

MY HEART SWELLS

and draws water from the air.
The wind, a wide
plate
around the sky. The land
calls out for miles.
These trees
are black filigree
pinned
to the wind. They twitch
like witchy signals
charged
with electric
sheets of rain.
Here, a delicate cobweb
contorts and dances in pink
spirals at my window frame. Later,
a field mouse
died an unearthly
death in the toilet, getting
caught in a rain it didn't
understand. And last night
in the attic an owl
crawled in and made lonesome
cool music all night.

        I don't know what to make of it.
        Things happen every day.
I'm glad.

HOW THE BLUE OF THE CHICKORY

is almost purple, how it floats,
see-through
in the grass
and flirts
like a liquid.
How threaded with sun.
How you fit
in the pocket
of this shadow
like a lock.
How the purple thistle
is a prickled
vase, an urn
of miracle
in this sparkled
field.
How?
How?
How
quickly the seasons pass.
How
little we know. How
the club-footed yellow
flowers puff and strut.
How the white
crowns
of Queen Anne's
lace laugh
in the grass.
How the field is countless
and full. How many
wands of chicory
lift
and wave?

REUNION

we sit in a circle
and talk. Together

our faces are a new
kind of moon. We give

each other back
to each other the same

but warmer,
changed by this shiny

new shape. We are
sharper, more vivid. We

wait for what each other
will say and laugh. We make

room for the words
in our laps

like warm nets.
We catch. We carry

limb to limb.
We're a wound

and we are wound
together, a round,

sure shape
stitched from the inside.

At ease, we let time
sit behind us, a tamed

monster we yawn
at and

dismiss. Later,
I watch the slow shape of the river crawl.

SHOULDER THROUGH

these tough August shadows. They're indigo, deep
as the word
indigo. Put your weight
into it. If you say ay *Ah-gust*
out loud
it sounds like dust,
like a fog
of dusty tree bark, soft
and green as a ghost
or creek rock
rolled
over slow
water, long stretches
of loosestrife relaxed
into purple
mattresses. The word August
is a river
of bends,
lengthy; it meandered
here
where the sand
ends.

THE BROKEN CHURCH

I walk beside the shuttered church. It's hot

    and July. There's Covid. The homeless people

are large purple shadows under the trees.

        The quiet breaks

        into two demolition crews

        across the street. Huge

        rusted shovels

        grab the dirt and eat

        at the hole. The groaning

        groans on. Many trucks hide

    behind shabby walls, disembodied.

So many

        unhoused humans

        asleep in shadows

        at noon under jackets

        at peace for now

        or at least

        in place. I keep walking,

careful

    not to intrude, my

footsteps

      quiet with them, blessing

    them.

WITNESS POEM

It's high time and past time
to write about the cat.

How we found him beside the garage.
His soft fur, the flies.

It's time to speak
of silent animal shapes

as the true shape
of all things

living, the shape of departure
and return,

designs of long space
and silence,

long space and time.
It's time to write about a lover,

the poem about the indent
left in the sand.

It's time to write about
she who drowned, she

who stopped, she who jumped, lost.
Time to write about the ledge

and menopause. The lookout,
the coupons

for spot remover, the degradation,
the look down, the stuck

in pubescence,
preschool, the intellect

left out. Time to write about a wildness,
a shame looking at

the good wife, the good mother,
the good witch.

It's time to write about guilt
and gardens. The one about the loud

hurting sounds of engines: how we're out-
numbered, hunted.

The one about 2-story
pickups, dark sides, menace.

The one about
eyesight and blurred

vision. The poem about failure
and regret.

The one about time
and the body, the indent

left in the sand. The poem about the beginning.
The one about silence, the opening

rooftops and
where the mind goes.

BECAUSE THE CLOTH

is made of threads,
because solidity

is an illusion
you can toughen up

the lines
and not lose the feel.

You can part company
and not be gone.

Because thread
is connective and moves

but comes apart
like a verb, a hitched

trailer bringing
everything along, I'd like the world

to give me time
to stir each moment

till the meaning thickens.
Stroked, cheered

and soothed
into new use.

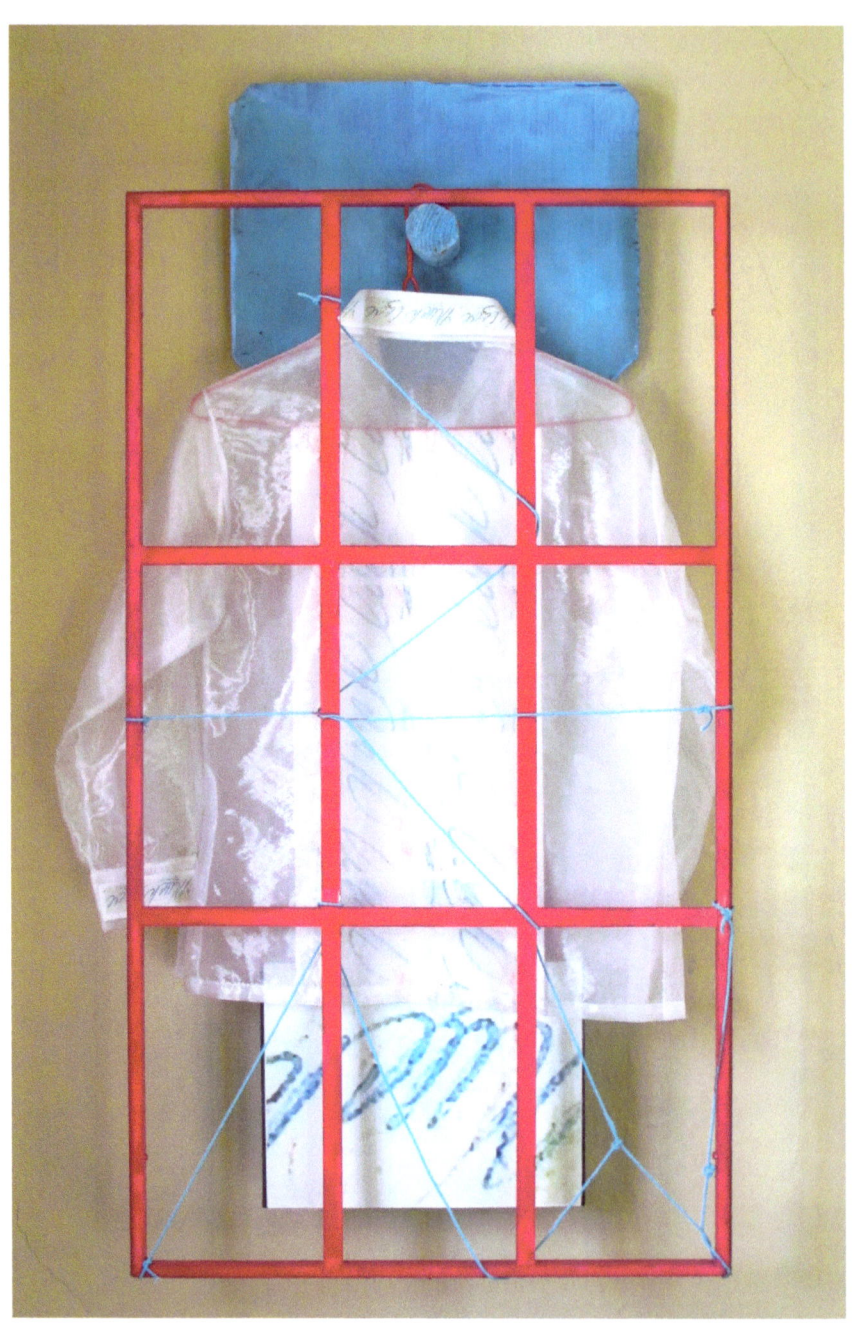

Up Close from a Distance, blouse, wrapped coat hanger, cord, photographed handwriting and wood

IS IT A WAVE OR A MUSCLE

Is it slick
loose water on the shore, fold
over fold, instinctively
just right? Does it
move like that? Seamless moon
opened up lily,
bottomless night?
Is there foam around it?
Or is it grittier
than that, more like the baseboards
in the bathroom, bills
to pay, month
after month, predictable
strain? The business
of being mortal together
strenuous, not shirking
from the tough spots? Rubbing
the imperfections
both ways, sensing
the rhythm. It may be a tree, un-separate
shade and sun.

GOLD'S GYM

is just around the corner.

ORACLE

*greatness in excess
dumbbells from any angle*

SUCCESS

if you take action
in all directions.

YIN   moving line: flowers
sprout from a rotting willow.

The beam is weak.

if you look for more support
you will regret it.

NO PRAISE
NO BLAME

SUMMER NIGHT

You want to
let the sweat smell
harden on you,
move
like a spice
through the air, move   move
like an equation, ingest
the air always
an accumulation
of all the
you, you are
always
a fermented
something
old, mysterious, sharp
as a ginger
        root.

THIS TONIGHT,
                    LUNGS full
    of turned, dark wind,
                        more bends,
        then my neck
            is a river
                    of diluted
            blue shadow
                    and streetlight
            flecked through
            the branches.
                EXPAND THIS
    sturdy woman
                    shaking
                    between the leaves
                    to swallow this wind-shaped
                        turn
                            into
            DREAM.

LIVING HERE

i

Outside, we walk
into the unsuspecting night.
The sky
is stiff as slate. Late
there's a moon. We stare at the edges
until our hearts break down.

ii

The trees are jet black
roots in reverse,
still as statues.
Are they going to speak?
They stand so still.
What do they seek?
Are they envoys of a world
we don't understand?
When we stop walking
they flood the sky with grief.

iii

The air is glass.
These nights the trees
have no tongues:
nothing warm.
The only sounds
are those of warning.

We haven't left yet.

Brother Suite

A suite of thirteen poems for

Chuck Webster,

*mandolin-playing, horse whispering, sonorous-voiced,
gentle brown-haired brother who died of brain cancer
on August 10, 2019, in Campbellsburg, Kentucky*

Is love a wing,
a sword, an enlarged
tent of comfort, a warm
want to stay, a pledge, a way
to close the gaps, the hurt, a way
to hold? All of this and more,
you opened us.

I TRAVEL A THOUSAND MILES

to sit in a room full of pot smoke and cigarettes, bluegrass
with my brother.
I travel to sit with the smoke
and the music and the tender
hands of the musicians
while the tumors
fight for space
in his brain.

I travel a thousand miles
to sit with my calm
brother, my sweet,
brown-haired brother. His mandolin
chords and the quiet tumors
in his head.

Bluegrass
and cigarette smoke.
Perfume
and poison
meet each other:
you are the same.

Same, the same.
Mandolin &
smoke.

DISMANTLED

Decreased
Disabled
Differently-
abled
      Swollen
      Fighting
      Different
            Loving
            Focused
            True
            No bullshit
            The big stuff
            Heart of it
                  No color
                  No color
                     in our eyes
                        they're the same
            all week
            I'm weak. Limp
                     color slides
                        from the window.

FOCUS

Speak

              Effort

                      What

I feel when I see him:
     Elated
     Relieved
     Arrived
     Overjoyed
     Overflowing
     Spilling
     I'm spilling
     What can I give?

Sit with him
     and his experience, listen.
   There's music. He plays
  his favorite
     app, pulls in
     soulful, smart songs
     that ache and climb. His choice.
     He can choose that. Choose and
     determine your music my
     beautiful
     brother. I'll sit
     with you
     and ask
     nothing.

GIVE ME A BRIEF SYNOPSIS. IT WAS BOTH

affable and
hard
the Spanish voices in the hall
overtook
then opened
at last
the cadence
in our hearts.
Broken
in the old hotel,
a torrent
of dirty water
toward
each of us, un-
chained
down the hall.   How
can a heart
    overflow
    and break at the same time?
    Some laughs.
    Breaking, I
    broke. Full of
    holding out   and   reaching
          toward
you.

HIS LAST SUMMER

Before the phrase
is fully formed

in my mind, I plow it under,
the "V" movement through the

subterranean soil of my emotions
covers and rejects it. I refuse.

Who knows how many summers
anyone has? A summer

is not a thing
that wants to be last. Swollen,

he was limping, living
on courage.

SONG OF UNDERSTANDING

I will write my brother a song of understanding, here
                              in the Vermont Department of
                              Motor
                              Vehicles. I will say
the word forgiveness once
                              for every person
                              in in this room.
                              I will say thank you
                              to this drafty place.
                              I'll say gratitude
in a wide way,

                              louder than before:
                              we are all waiting

                              to be brothers and sisters
                              in the same room.
                              Especially thank you
                              to the woman next to me who said

"There should be more than one stall in a place like this."

              Earlier, my husband
              touched my hand and I believed

              he knew the weeds
              in me, and I relaxed

              as everyone in this room
              deserves to do. As everyone's eyes speak

              beyond words.

How many bonds are enough?
Now,
from a thousand miles away, in the
      Department of Motor Vehicles, my
      brother
      with cancer hands me his calm
      and his easy
      way of down play. He
      reaches past his disease
that outreaches
all disease
to comfort me. The importance
of calm
    cannot be overestimated.

    Loyalty too, once thought
    to be too still
    or buttoned up

    turns out to be more like a loose ribbon
    than a button. I gave

him a ribbon
    to get in. My darling brother,
    who busted my sandcastle
    as a toddler

is a castle
of *now* but he's changing.

He changed. I changed. How important

to change and be clear,

    like him, the
    sound
    of sand and affection
    endures.

PICKIN' PARTY

Dave and I fly
in from Vermont on flight #609.
Excited, I pour
coffee for the circle
of Kentucky musicians who plop
a shot of bourbon in their cups
for good luck. We settle in next to Kenny.
He strokes his long beard and smiles.
Nephew, Patrick's earnest
face is full of questions.
My sister closes her eyes and rests
her tuning hand on the bass string.
My brother's wife smiles
a tired smile from the outer circle.
Sully nods, and the music starts.
Chuck's gleaming mandolin lays like a child on his lap,
massaged and stroked with his swollen
good hand. Head bent as though
deep listening was the mission
of his life. Designs of Marlboro
smoke swirl overhead. Chuck manages
a puff or two. The warm grey fumes say
what the hell? The sweet aroma's
not unlike his horses' hay in the field.
Six string guitars, washtub bass, twelve
string guitar, and a magical maraca. Lynn
lifts us with her steady beat
and focused attention.
The players pick their brains
for another tune, then another:
*Foggy Mountain Breakdown, My Cumberland Plateau,
The Sunny Side* - a different rendition
every time. The circle holds back time

while any distrust of outsiders
is smoothed and sung around
by common love for this beautiful man
who is dying, full of song and cheer
for a man who is living.

MY BROTHER CHUCK

is the only person
who ever noticed or commented on the thick scar
on he underside of my upper right arm.

Evidently you hurt it…
he said a few years before he died. *Evidently*
was one of the words
he used that I loved the most.
Evidently, he was the only person I knew who used
that word.

The world presents much
that is evident
but usually we
don't notice. Chuck
noticed. We shared the chaos
of our teenaged
home, busting
at the seams, five of us,
too fast, too
loud, too much. That scar.

My twelve-year-old arm plunged
through a window to make the haste
go away. No one

there except Mom who rushed
me to the tiny ER where
someone drew sloppy stitches through the wound.
I can see them today
on the tender, underside flesh
of my arm,
raised skin

where the string went through.

What does it take for a brother to notice a wound?
He did.

CHUCK SAID I NOTICED THINGS

that no one else did. He liked that.
When Mom and Dad died
he gathered up every speck of good
bad indifferent
artwork from crannies, walls, attic, storage space,
of our childhood home
and quietly,
urgently packaged them
up and shipped them to Vermont and me
many states away. I can picture him,
long legged shuffle, serious concentration, clear focus on
the mission
at hand. For dear life,
for me.

A SOLUTION

He said he had a solution
for the blazing sun
in my face that summer
in Kentucky when he was dying.

That's what he said while he limped
toward the striped
canvas of his porch awning
to unspool
the cover above my head.

My brother was looking for solutions.
 We'd spoken
of his specific symptoms
and daily details
of life and disease.
I'd asked him what he thought a particular
solution might be. Now
he echoed
my use of the word "solution."

"I have a solution," he said, eager to move
toward a problem
where there was solution.
Limping sideways
to the pulley
and the handle, his
exaggerated
slow gait grabbing. Willed
intention
behind every move.

What pleasure and sublime grace
to receive
and hold
the swaying
awning
where he placed it
safely away
from my head.

A solution.

GREEN PEPPERS

were a solution too. With his shaky hand
Chuck ordered a pizza
on the app on his phone
for the whole family

He took tremendous pride in
providing this service for us.
He took orders
from each of us, but chemo and
his disease made his hands shake
and his eye fuzzy. He hit
hot peppers instead of green peppers.
They were the best hot peppers that I couldn't eat
of my whole life.

FOREVER

frozen
and sacred, the
moment he reached for me
over the phone
days before he died.
It was FaceTime.
He couldn't speak, but his hand
grabbed for the screen
of the iPhone
held out in Kentucky.
It brought me to him.
The flesh of his hand
filled the camera lens
with a beautiful blur
as it turned
toward me.
He wasn't able to say "This
looks like the end," though he
may have thought it
reaching toward me.

Our faces and time
frozen in that stupid
little screen. The miracle of being with him.
The concrete way
he wanted to touch it. Did he think I was there? I was
and I wasn't but oh I want that he thought
I was.

ANOTHER FACETIME

I puzzled
and fretted
over what his lips mumbled
to tell me. "I'm suffering?"
"Save me?" "I love you?"
His effort distorting
what may have been tender
or not. O
God
let me know.

YES, BUT I'M WADING

in darkness, sometimes, I'm floating
thigh-high in danger, waiting
for a signal
from an invisible pool.
I'm waiting for a deeper,
true swallowing.
I want to put something in my pocket
that says balance.

DECEMBER

It's December, brother,
here on earth in neighborhoods

without you. It's the darkest month
down here. Where are you?

The neighborhood's sealed
in ice, brother.
Where are you? Dark seams

pull the grim houses
tight, braced for another go.

Are you loose
now, in your warmth and

characteristic calm, free
of Decembers?

Do you laugh
where you are

and lounge in your chair?
Can you see me

and my reach, desperate
to keep you here?

The streets
have turned to ice, brother.

It's night. The children bring flashlights
to find you, fingers

bruised and shadowed
with questions. Their hearts glow

in December dark. Our
tabletop candles simmer

in their syrupy surfaces,
weak light without you.

Don't forget us, brother. Our houses
remember your name, warm

with your name.

Chuck and Sharon

Sentinels

MAKE A NEW

You there, moving in the yard, natural
as a shadow
or a shred
of grass – relaxed

with the tawny
creatures who flit
through the changing light

and yearn. I am
nothing

but I am grateful.
How many times

are you willing to pull things apart?
How many times
will you feel

for what's under the surface
        with hope
and with need?

Birth of Idea Totem, oil and watercolor crayon

INSTEAD OF THE FUNERAL

the paintings: the rich urge
of them, the hungry
human heart of them.
Eye-made, hand-
held   color. Instead

of the funeral,
        the sky / opened in hoops
and hoops
of steel blue and gray.
The thought of what's possible.

Instead of the funeral
the sunset, a hundred shades
of pink this average evening,
then blue, generous
and gradual. Instead

of the funeral, someone's
shoulder, a thin ripple of wind
in the hem of a dress, a row
of windows / picking up light,
        red berries in winter, night
        spilling in the street.

        Unabashed, eye to eye.   Instead

of the funeral, some music.
The exertion of the hill,   the best
        part at the top, the hard
        regular gift
        of having to push.

Instead of the funeral
a whole breath, unashamedly

notice
        how it goes.

ANOTHER COLD EASTER, REACHING

the eternal empty

as I
laugh.

Let's cancel Easter.
Without entering, walk

toward the harsh wind at Trader Joe's. Then

turn around and walk out.

Medallion, books, glass surface, satin, brass nails

SINCE MY MOTHER DIED

she's taken up residency
here,
in my
left hand.
She's re-
shaped it
completely: her
long fingers on my cup,
her loopy grasp
on the water faucet,
her sensitive aches. And when I
look in the mirror, where she lives now
too, I say out loud, Oh, Mom!
bewildered by this change of address,
her visitation here,
and our long unfinished
walk together.

Step by Step, acrylic paint

SENTINELS

I'm giving myself
this day of remembrance,
this holy day of forgetting. The song,

Pressure Drop, plays
over and over
in my head. There
is my first vivid memory:

I'm three years old
on top of a sandy embankment
watching the waves
at my feet, saying,
out loud and triumphant, "They can't get me from here."

There is no way around it.
Some things were hard. When my mother
drove her car into the Ohio River it was devastating,

but triumphant
too. So decisive
for a woman who, at the time
was unsure
of everything.
Everything: frozen peas
or frozen carrots
or whether to keep
living. But the thing is
you couldn't blame her.
The way things were, no choice
looked that good.

And the water *was* shallow
where she went in
and it was the heart of town
with people around. So maybe,

as the wife of a mayor, what she did
was closer to performance art,
to say fuck all this,
precise
eloquent. Who knows?

But when I found out last winter
that Lizzie tried to kill herself
when the bombs
were dropping
and the temperature
wouldn't go
above zero, after

the comforting words I said
Adrienne Rich's words:
"Every woman's death diminishes
me." "Yeah,"
Lizzie said, "but
they enrich me too."

I didn't know
what she meant
then, but now I think maybe
she meant the spirits

of those women stay
on as sentinels

to warn us. Snagged
on human
terrain during
their violent passage. Stay

on as ghosts
who say: Not
this way. Turn back.
Not. Not. Not.

Pay attention
to what isn't

whole yet. I am watching the waves
fold into themselves.
I am saying, slowly
and without words,
"They can't get me from here."

MY MOTHER AND I APPROACH

the trunk of family photos the same way:
with equal parts awe
and terror.
We fear
that we will never surface
from its formless pull.

We know it is powerful,
jumbled and impossible to order.
We know
the trunk is a puzzle
with no solution, no final answer, no closure.
We know, too, that we will feel compelled
to try anyway.

I love this about my mother
and understand it as a secret pact. I know
it is a secret pact
so I feel less alone
in my trepidation

The trunk is enormous and overfull. Ancient metal
with rusty hinges, two feet deep, long
like a treasure-shaped coffin. The trunk says
there's nothing to do but surrender
though we fight it.
We fight it. My mother and I approach the family photos
        like crime scenes -
        earnest for clues,
        deceptions or patterns. Why?

       Who? When?
   What was on the mantle?
   the table? What party?
   Who's guilty? Who's not? What need
   bleeds among square after square
   of buried narrative? Some

photos have frames,
most don't, some are huge,
or tiny, ripped duplicates.

There is another trunk in the next room.

THE HEAT OF MENOPAUSE

The heat of menopause
is on my cheek; a buzz
of blood and hormones
brightens my skin.
I'm in a parked car
overlooking a valley
of trees with a good view.
My mother did this too,
seeking peace and solitude.
So I have a question.
How is the fizz
of this process
less womanly
than the womb's
monthly flow
or the hold of the fetus
in its pocket?
Unless she dies young,
every woman will know it.
When did the shame get in?
When and where
did the fear
get in?
Fear of the hag
and the crone. Fear
of the *hideous. Hideous*
is a word my mother
used too often to describe herself.
The root word of hideous is *hide*
so as not to be appalling
to others.
Of course, it was always about the others.
But what
if the delicate
pink on my cheek
is a gift of ripeness and arrival?
A new sensuality and warm welcome
to a good view.

Little Kells Room, mixed media

SKIN

Natural sponge grows on the ocean floor in Tarpon Springs, Florida. Greek sponge divers settled there in the early 1900s, creating a booming, eclectic industry and culture. My partner and I visited this unusual town while Covid brewed in secret.

Day 1

I discover my skin
in the Florida cottage. Take off
thick layers of air
travel, long
sleeves of shuttled, rushed
and pushed to uncover
the pale skin
of my New England body.
Look, look
I'm the mermaid on the poster,
scales on my arms and legs,
torso alive and
swimming
in the bedsheets.
Who's the tourist now?

Day 2

The breeze
has slackened offshore.
The Greek men's
somber glances
so close to my face as they speak
are less obtrusive
than when they just stare. That
glare. A fit
of sun and shadow
makes short work
of the surface.

Day 3

A stiff wind
at our backs
gussies up the bayou,
shifts the fronds in the palmetto trees. Split
sunlight
twists on the bedsheets.
The wall
flickers,
a kiss
of yes
and
no.

Day 4

Prickly dreams
taste the same as the drawn-out garlic
on my tongue, a
trapped dawn inside me
punches at 2 am. Dreams
prolong
the
wait.

Day 5

Cold for Florida:
Freeze warnings
endanger the un-
suspecting Hibiscus plants, alarm
the salamanders
and strangers. We too,
are confused.
The wind
stiffens the coconut trees, Spanish
moss tossed like packing string
all over the lawns. Succulent stems
droop in sad Octopus arms.
I fold my arms in bed,
a sphinx
of in and out,
a map
of my own
lost direction.

Day 6

Bayou. Let's stay
on that word. Its sound:
Bye you, Bay yoo. Bi-you. And
its meaning -- smooth
fist of sea, a slick
blister.
The backs of dolphins
rise and fall, rise and fall
and I am still.

Day 7

We are tender
and remember the decent
'shoulds.' The open
questions. The docks
where the divers go, piles
of sponges, such useful
barnacles, treasure and
oily garbage.
Below that
the smell of gasoline
puts us in our place.
Gold
on the water
flouts
the land where our jobs
wait.

RAINCLOUD

When the rain comes, suddenly
I'm primal and old

as the knuckled air
that beats my bones. It happens

every time the thunder
moves those huge,
engorged muscles

like inky spleens
through the ruptured sky.

     I press my nose to the dirt
        and sniff

the safe, soft ground. My belly moves
with the convulsing air. The tips

of my fingers are ten
        true rituals

        small moons
        strung together

        like beads
        or impossible orbits.

My lungs fill with dark chants and clouds.

        I taste destruction
        on my lips oh
            god of wrath
        god of anger
        you are erect
        in the burgeoning air.

I praise you, I acknowledge
       your power and the pure
   dread that fills me. The
             taste is sweet
       as the first
                   rain
                       drop

ALL NIGHT THE MOON

ran high
in the arched mouths

      of the hot
      dry
      lilies. I
stashed survival
in my teeth
by laughing
      all night the moon
      ran, a wet
      fold in the hot
      dry lilies.

All night   the moon   the earth
ripened   the floor   of the sky

      with slick
      new blossoms.

MAY THIRD

has space around it, unafraid
with strong legs
and purple sunglasses.
The car windows
bring in real
breathable air. The kind of open
that doesn't mean danger
or pain. The sounds
that come in are not
signals
of distress. There's
a bird,
a call
of imminent pleasure.
My Mamma
done told me it's
ok but
wiggly in paradise. Paradise has to be chipped away at
to feed
its ongoing
need. There's a place
for you, she said, looking up
from the bottom of the stairs. Her voice
a song that carried
a path
to the song.

Rolling Pin Song, mixed media

MAYBE THIS PARKING LOT

beside the Kinney drugstore
will be my summer vacation.

The asphalt's warm
and exhilarating,
made of 4 rivers
          of moving air just like Babylon

on my arm. The birth
      of civilization
      up my shoulder.

Because of this parking lot, I have a boarding pass
              to time
              abroad / a door to more

      time to wonder
      and stumble
      into what the Celts called "the *entrelacs*,"
   the time between the
time.
      I've waited for this stew
      of weeds
      beside the car
      for a long time.
      I've longed for this exit
   sign and these
unnameably
   tangled trees
by the gas station.

      My bags are packed
with fully-
      formed trees that
      retreat
      into themselves
      with me.

I CARRY A YELLOW

rectangle of air
to the tossing blue lake.

The long water's stretched
loose

and beckoning
as Venus's welcoming pool

of birth and beginning.
Parking lot to grass,

grass to sand, I carry that
floating device under my arm.

Under my sundress, my spine
aches for the occasion.

"Don't put your blanket there!
Ants!!" a woman barks loud

when I spot a good place
under a tree. She looks up

from her card game to disapprove
and glare. Recovering, I breathe

in the scene.
No wimpy puddle, but huge raucous

chops of water.
I feel the grit of sand

and slosh under my feet.
Gulls squawk

their beautiful discontented "Awwck!!"
Leaves bubble

and swoosh in the windy currents. Groups
of African men

gather on the grass, excited
with the clink and clatter

of a game of ring toss.
Large families sport

colorful clothes
and scarves that gleam against their perfect dark skin.

Closer to the water, young women
with slick stomachs

and bare butts
stand proud with thongs in their cracks.

A different, tall woman stands erect, sturdy as Demeter
at the edge of the water.

She moves with perfect posture
to throw a ball to her dog and kids.

Tiny waves lick her shins. (Omg,
that's my physical therapist! No wonder

she stands so straight.) A budding
'tween romance plays out: two young guys

muster the courage to approach
a couple of barely-'tweened

girls with caramel-colored skin.
They ask eloquently, "Whatcha doin?"

"Swimmin," one girl responds.
Though she isn't. She's standing

on the sand in her bikini absently
cradling a cell phone. "Don't drown!"

one guy calls and they hurry off,
nothing left to say.

A couple in their 70's sit
on aluminum beach chairs. She reads a book

with great focus
in the sun while he sleeps

farther back in the shade.
When she walks

back towards him, he looks up and says
slowly, "You look so beautiful."

She bows her head to blush
and brushes him off,

changes the subject.
A few seconds later, she takes his hand.

Are these rituals a communal
coming to the trough? Mammals

around water in their necessary
playground? Maybe this platter

of rippled silver is God:
the platform

on which everything else depends. The frolic
put back into the madding crowd.

Satisfied, I squash
my yellow rectangle of air

under my arm and head home.

THE SUITCASE

After the pat down
at security, I put on my jacket
and forget
my suitcase at the gate.
So unraveled
by my father's dying,
states away, I don't notice
till just before take-off.

I run for the attendant and clutch
her arm:
"Help me,"
I say, "my father
is dying."
"He's dying," repeating in case
she didn't hear.
She winces
and looks down.
"My arm," she says flatly.
We find the suitcase just in time.

When the plane lands in Philly,
I lose it again. Look
at a text from the hospital
and leave it
in the breezeway with stowed bags. Just walk
right past it. After
hoofing fast, fast, fast
through grey corridors halls
for what feels like
miles for a tight connection, I realize
it's gone again!
Ashamed
of my inefficient
brain and thinking he would be too,
I run.
Run like I have never run. Run like a lion's chasing me, run

till my lungs
are nothing but *"HUH… !! HUH…! !HUH…!!"*
hot and panting, run till the pain
wipes out thought, and I'm nothing
but effort.
If he must die, I
must die with him. I must
exhaust my heart and lungs to reach him. I must pushmy
lungs into dust
& reincarnation so that I can give them back to him
so that he will live.
If I run fast enough…if I run fast enough
if I run fast enough
I can save him.

Drenched, my skin
burning,
I reach the plane just in time, flames
in my lungs.
At the hospital,
my siblings and I sit around my father's bed,
protecting him - a fortress
of willed-wellness and stability. We have never
seen so many machines, pumps and tubes. His blood moves
by the grace of God and medical
genius. He breathes through a wide pipe.
We tell stories. The sound of each other's voices comforts us
a bit and Dad hears. He relaxes a little. His facial expressions
carry us on waves of love and grief.

We each say thank you in our ways, which means
(though we can't bear to think it) goodbye. We cry.

He slips away after we leave for the night. The nurses tell us
it's often that way. Did we each carry a piece of his soul
as we trundled to bed? Very late, did we catch his spirit
on its way?

The suitcase is delivered after Dad's gone. Days later,

I'm shocked
to still be here
alone with my suitcase
with the ache
in my chest
and air in my lungs.

AUGUST

IS LIKE THAT.   AFTERWARDS

things   go to seed
                   or fruit. What's
                            left is after-

        image:
                   the weeds
                   and the disabled
                   people. Someone
                   typing from across
                   the road. An open
                            window. When
                            you close your eyes

        the smell of extra seed and weeds

        fill up the entrance.

August   is like that   folding

        over   the sound of cicadas   and the
                   silence
                            afterwards.

LAST NIGHT ALL MY DEAD PETS CAME BACK

tiny shrunken dachshunds the size of grocery store weenies,

balled-up baby hamsters, shimmery goldfish,

the cat with those flat

mushroom-like appendages

hanging from her fur. She's full of nettles

and eye infection. But Dave says,

"If we clean her up, she might get venereal disease + die."

Like the tumors kept her alive. This is a dream, remember.

The tumors kept her alive.

Then I'm pulling on the end of a pillar of blue play-dough.

A young person holds the other end. Eventually, I end up

in a swimming pool with a lump

of intestinal blue dough in my hands. I hear

a voice say, "If you join a church, you'll

have more energy. This potion may help! This prayer!"

Then my cousin says, "But you don't _do_

large dinner parties, do you?"

Which meant that it was my own fault

that my life hadn't turned out better. "But

there are _lots_ of people here," I say as I go downstairs to hide.

Then another voice speaks of the success

of strangers, "Just look

how tidy her paintings are! She had potion. Prayer."

But I eye the stiff garment bags in the hall and think,

"Not my religion."

CLOSE TO AUTUMN,

a red smear pulls away
from the trees.
I watch as the red smear
becomes a red t-shirt,
and then a young woman.
The echo of her
organized footfall
thrums:
        beat,
        beat,
          beat
off the pavement.
A steady
        huff
        huff
          huff

rises in the ravine,
and blooms
from her lungs
seamless
pockets of respiration
echo and grow
enormous beside the lake. I give her my locked
attention and praise
for her moving lungs,
two feet and one
mind that insists on pushing
past the vast
momentum of inertia and decay.
She's everyone
who struggles next to bullies
of pain, war, anxiety.
Next to
huge boulders and trees, a speck
in the vortex of seasons, poised
at the beginning
and close to autumn

SPILLED BIRDSEED

My old winter boots slip
   on the slick
   fallen snow which in turn tips
   a 5-pound bucket
   of birdseed
      while I laugh hard.
      Out rushes
   a multitude of multi-colored
   seeds on the squinting
   white surface. Tiny
      golden nuts, sweet millet and black
   sunflower shells
      spill like ice cream sprinkles
   on stiff winter hide.
   Oh, accidental flow! Oh, giddy
   seeds newly free
   on the nutty ground! An orgy
   for what flies
      or burrows. This February
   I'm dumping it all,
        holus-bolus,
   unmeasured
      and kissing
      the low-lipped sun.
          Oh, sweet pleasure
          of last-ditch light
          Oh, delicious weight
      of spilled seed. The feel
      of release more real
      than what's held.

Branches

THREADED TREES

Threaded Trees was a solo dance choreographed and performed by movement artist and teacher, Sara Mcmahon. Bill Davis wrote the beautiful music.

In September,

Sara's pulsing gestures:

arms extended

into saxophone's wail,   waving goodbye, hello

a river of feeling

from my friend's eye

at such a long wave. Memory

knotted under dark,

glossy water.

The lit-up look

on a watcher's face. The best part

is the long reach, Sara's arm

still reaching/ longing

for what's not

or what is the roll of the moon, its husk

on the water. I wish

the water and I   were that seed

all the time. The best

story I ever heard

was real

serious.   Like water,

you're memory.

Squint your eyes
     and the yellow flowers are instant
     runny Monets. Oh,
     your slim arm
     is another branch
     in the backyard sunlight.
     The bare place leaves me helpless
     to say anything. It's
     all changed somehow everyone
     moves like a sonnet.
     How much
     sun adds up to air?

          ~

The cats tie up the neighborhood with wild, fevered jumps
through ripped greens and
back porches. The cats
invent their journey
with x-ray vision
and sense of smell.
Their long
muscles
invent the shadows.

          ~

     The sound in my skull is almost as good
     as the sky / breaking
     on the side of the house.
     Almost as good
     as the rain softening
     the bends
     of my veins. The moon
     is wide open
     and reminds me
     of everything
     that hasn't happened and
     has.

~

Dusk

Slight purple
mixed with night
the time before night
the light within night

~

We were always writing
            with pens that were running
out of ink. We were falling
leaves and sparrows.
We always fell in circles.
Which is feather, which is leaf?
We were always close,
but never done.

~

She watches him
through the rotting wood
of the old window.
He is smoking. The air
is hot. Outside, the leaves make a slow
shuffling sound
like paper
turning over. The leaves are dreaming.
He studies them.
She studies him.
They both want to know
is there still time?

~

I'm glad that the darkness
has sifted
into the crotches,
of these gentle trees. Their "V"s
open
to collect
the falling shadows.

~

The sound of the ocean is part silence
       part roar,
       part pause
       and slow-motion
       fall.
       A question is at the crest.

~

FROM THE UPSTAIRS

APT.

    oh no   here

come those   cherubs   again.   once

a monk   always:

        sanctify
        sanctify
        sanctify.

it's just that
        goddamn david rohn
        & his concertos again.

        the ceiling is not
        melting in clouds, closing
        in chorus
        or the judgement at hand.

                he's up there painting
                    the work

is dangerous

            disorganized

                 gets

            louder.

YOU SPEAK TO ME AND I BREATHE

      the sea
      through your mouth. I taste

the color of coral on my tongue
                and feel the slick
bevel of fishes.
You smooth the way. Now

the air is water and
      we float. The room
fills up with pearls.

      You make the
      dark within me
capsize and run
      like rain through a tunnel and

      for a time
      we are together
      on the
      round, round earth.

Portrait of Dave, watercolor and mixed media

A TRICK

with Wagner   for effect/

early   summer   bare   ly

summer . . .

compare

it   to music.

stuff it.

catch it on your tongue   like   a

like   a

~~like   a~~

lichen

is the green stuff

that grows

where it's usually

too hard.

Wagner

is good

to compare   it to   who

ever   he was   must've

been something

I missed.

SHE SENT ME A MESSAGE IN A BOTTLE

filled with the tactile details
of her life
while her body stood outside,
a plug,
tense and demanding.

She sent me a message that bloomed,
a thing apart, un-
wrapped and longing. She
loosened, she drifted,
she fell
apart like dry petals.

She unveiled.

She opened.

She smoothed the shards of her strictly
dictated script and sent it
because it was short.

She sent me.
She revealed.

She sent me a message in a bottle
with a code
of longing inside

while her body waited.

THE SAXOPHONE

     wiggles
   this hot Friday night,

long blue noise, hard
    yellow horns,

     slick shine
on the surface

     of this last blue
     ripped

day of June. The sound
    slithers and the skin

of your knees moves
    under your jeans.

WHAT WAS IT LIKE

when you and he, can you describe what it was like?
Well, there was light.
I remember the light.
It was green and falling
slant-
wise, it was cool. Yes, the light
had a life of its own. And it fell repeatedly. It kept on;
it was transparent.
I could say iridescent. Yes,
it was smooth. The closest I can get
is eucalyptus
leaves, green. There were his arms
cool, his chest. There
was his stomach,
thighs. Warm
but cool, soft but firm. Inscrutable
like the moon-skinned
surface of sleek
new leaves.
Cool light, slanted fall.
No, I can't say what it was like at all.

CROWS

BLACK BIRDS

you're a clutter

of black feathered cups, a squawk

of comments, all dark

flutter and fluff, you sit

at the tips of stripped winter trees. Moving,

you amuse me. Puff

and puff, awk! awk! awk!

I salute your squeaky pulse

while you turn

and dance

just in time.

A TREE CRIES

full of crows. A pyramid
of ice, night
of feathers. It's Friday
and February. Each
branch is an echo
of an echo
of a call
for help.
Call! Call! Call!
for food
for warmth,
for others. Each call is different and the same.
This mountain-
sized tree
is an armor
of pitch-colored birds and communal shine.
May I address you directly, black
bodies?
You're slick as the knife
of this minus 20
degree air.
You are not a murder
you're life
because you know pain. You're everyone's
horror and everyone's strength.
When you fall
on the loaf
of bread
I toss at the base
of the tree
all at once, you
are the same wing.

16 Crows/A Tree Cries, installation, nylon fabric, latex paint, wood.

This visual art installation was born at the same time as the poem, A TREE. The collective energy of cold, hungry birds and that of humans struck me as very much the same and inspired this mixed media piece. Words of the poem are written on each perched "crow." Shown here at The SPACE Gallery in Burlington, Vermont

A TREE

cries through
the night,

swollen
with
crows

heavy,
moving

dark
calls, all

or nothing,
ten-

below, thousands
of black

iced feathers
gleam.

Their need
for heat

and food
is sacred

and communal.
Scarcity

made solid

by all,

all, all! That
noise

is
music

for
survival.

MIGRATION

A wobbly
line of tough-assed crows
                        fights like hell
                                against a
                November sky. I watch
them push
back walls of wind
and freezing ice:
back
back
back
until their glossy
                wings
                are ripped black
                flags that
                flap and flap.
                        They throw themselves
                        hard
                        into the
                battered sky. Without

pity, the winds
                                push but black
                                row upon row

of loopy crow
lines push harder. The bird

                in front strings
                them along till their lines split
                and spill

like loose ink through the sky, til their "V"
formations
become "U"

formations, then
just torn
threads. My heart aches

to watch them. *Heart ache*
is an old phrase, but it fits.

My muscles
strain with them. Abruptly slack,
then fighting back
into
formation.

I do not know
what makes them struggle
to find order against all chaos,
and odds,
but it is radiant
and makes
my breath catch: The need to be with others
and claim
the unraveling
design behind designs:

I've been where the air's raw
with that urge and that hell
bent.

PARTING

MAKE THE BED LIKE A PRAYER

a book of white
leaves, a sleeve
of forgiveness. Move the sheets
like a promise,
a portal
of hope between
now
and before, a shuffled
stairway, a memory.
A hymn to *care*
and to
need,
to the fold
between the fold.

OBLONG

                         patches of

          pewter-colored ice

                    along the road, hard

     patterns

               on the lake.   sweet)

haze, an ache.

          the sky

                    opens,   an applause

          of low birds

                    & wings.

Lift, wood block, photo, sheet music

THE THING ABOUT A HOUSE

or
How Many Things Happen After We Give Up

I.

Mom died then Dad so
we had to sell the house in Kentucky where

I grew up with my four siblings. In some ways,
losing the house
was a loss

as violent and confusing as losing my parents.

If these walls could talk
they'd speak the language of dust,

beginning
and
forever.

Dust. Growth. Trauma. Vines

grew right through a crack in the window sill in an upstairs
bedroom
one August, way

out into the room like a disembodied arm.
I called my partner in Vermont:

"It's creepy!" Too much growth
seething there
for one person to hold.

II.

Nothing is as complex
and full of ladders,

going in and going out, as a house.

As our house,
exactly somewhere
between a tobacco field and suburbia.

Exactly not either.

III.

Time itself
lived in that house

with its blank face
and automatic gestures.

Its soft lap
and its motion sickness, its tacit

understanding
that there would be time

to solve,
to venture, to plan, or escape.

IV.

The thing about a house is that it reflects

a time and the people of a time
in a more

detached, deeper, subjective, unswayed way

than a single person in one moment
ever could.

These walls know conflicts, worries, resolutions, memories.

Here, my handwriting gets eerily like my mother's, with the same
underlinings.

A house does the work of holding
so we can look away

V.

and look back. A séance
of candles & shrines in the living room,
silver and chartreuse.

'Chartreuse' in the dictionary is a pale green
or yellow liqueur. Perfect! Mood,

music, mirrors, revelry. Mom's
favorite chair in the corner,

cigarettes by the window. Her open face over a book,

private and full
and oh,

how she exhaled!
Dad's childlike

naked feet padding into the kitchen.
How he breathed

in the air of new evening
on the back porch with the deep cricket

pulse and the swollen night,
his thoughts

filling the shape of the room,
soothing the gnarls of history.

Growing and coming
to rest.

VI.

But don't smooth it out too much. The house
has cheap plastic

flooring & the color of the rug is puke
green, not chartreuse.

It has shorelines of grime and fatigue,
fraught chapters

that chase fast after the gentle ones. Truth
is beauty, don't
forget.

But never mind, new seasons
came in every year, surprising,
and clear.

Triumphs and simple pleasures

lined up under the roof like its people
and were undeniable.

Seven souls roamed these rooms,
pushing out,
being held. Verbs, routines, context.

VII.

The oak out back is taller now and more brittle.

Some branches have fallen, some endure,
markers of time,

complex
and full of ladders,

leaning in and leaning out.

The vines are quiet and unhurried;
their green skin

covers, reveals.

O SONG THAT PULLED THIS WETNESS

from my eye,
   this tear
smeared
   with grey feathers
   when doves
         lift quick

   at the window,
stirred by reasons
   of their own. Sight

   and sound
   kissed. That shift
   is music too.

It dislodges
everything.

This tear
belongs to them/
him/her

and our moving
surprixe

This blur/
   That turn
toward the window
     is for joy

Wing Song, chiffon, thread

About the Author

Sharon Webster is a poet, visual artist, and teacher of adults with cognitive challenges. Her work addresses the personal, celebrates the sensual, and believes in the mysteries of process.

Born in a colorful river town in Carrollton, Kentucky, Sharon has lived in Burlington, Vermont with her husband, the poet David Cavanagh, since 1982.

Webster is a frequent exhibitor of mixed media artwork in Vermont and elsewhere. She gives poetry readings whenever she is asked. Sharon is a big fan of the connection and chemistry of in-person poetry and art events for the shared experience they provide.

Sharon worked for more than thirty-five years with developmentally challenged people, helping them to lead rich, normal lives, teaching them art as well (though she often felt they were teaching her). She does this work now on a volunteer basis. Sharon taught Studio Art and research and fundamental writing for Burlington College and Community College of Vermont in Winooski, Vermont.

Her first book of poems and art, *Everyone Lives Here*, was published in 2014 by Fomite Press in Burlington, VT. A third book has been promised by Salmon Poetry in Ireland.

Sharon's website @sharonwebster.com

Writing a review on social media sites for readers will help the progress of independent publishing. To submit a review, go to the book page on any of the sites and follow the links for reviews. Books from independent presses rely on reader-to-reader communications.

For more information or to order any of our books, visit:
fomitepress.com/our-books.html

More poetry from Fomite...
Warren Baker
  Shadow Light
Anna Blackmer
  Hexagrams
L. Brown
  Loopholes
Sue D. Burton
  Little Steel
Christine Butterworth-McDermott
  Evelyn As
  The Spellbook of Fruit and Flowers
David Cavanagh
  Cycling in Plato's Cave
  Please Hold
Rajnesh Chakrapani
  The Repetition of Exceptional Weeks
James Connolly
  Picking Up the Bodies
Benjamin Dangl
  A World Where Many Worlds Fit
Greg Delanty
  Behold the Garden
  Loosestrife
Mason Drukman
  Drawing on Life
J. C. Ellefson
  Foreign Tales of Exemplum and Woe

www.ingramcontent.com/pod-product-compliance
Lightning Source LLC
Chambersburg PA
CBHW040845120626
46547CB00001B/35